pastel
hearts

kimmy ann

ISBN: 9781087223698

To the one reading this,

I hope you rediscover the magic of love in these pages.

INTRODUCTION

I wrote this book for me, and for you; for anyone who believes in love, wants to believe in love, or is struggling to believe love; and for anyone who has a broken heart, a healing heart, a cheerful heart, or a hardened heart. I pray my words reach your mind and touch your soul.

When life gets difficult, people tend to build fortresses around their heart to project themselves while they heal. The problem is, people stay there. They live there. They become depressed, angry, bitter, and hard. Pastel Hearts is named such to remind you, even though it's okay to experience negative feelings, to keep your heart soft and don't stay stuck.

I know it is very easy to speak of hope when you are writing from a place of peace and with a whole heart. That's where I was a little over a year ago when I first finished writing Pastel Hearts. However, recent events – loss of family members, friendships, and a love I thought would be my forever – made it difficult for me to publish the book as it was. I felt like a hypocrite. Here I was telling you how wonderful love is, that you'll overcome, and that everything would be okay when I didn't feel any of those things myself.

So, two weeks before this was to go to print, I re-wrote it. Part of me needed to prove I could still write about optimism, love, and hope when I wasn't feeling it. The purpose of this book is to show you that, despite the lies hurt and fear tell you, hope, happiness and love can always be found.

She was mesmerized
with how love
effortlessly danced
on the gold and green
pigments in his eyes…

… similar to the way
sunlight delights itself
on a stained-glass window.

- stained-glass -

If forever passes
and our lives never intersect,
I want you to know
I've met you every night
in my dreams and
fell in love with you
each time.

- dreamer -

I want to be
your daydream obsession,
the voice in your head
that you can't drown out.

- obsession -

I imagine being in love
is like holding all of heaven
in your heart at once —
overwhelming but oh so glorious.

- glorious -

Why do you only show the world
a puddles worth of all you are?

You are not a typical day
or small talk to fill the silence.

No.

You're multiple dimensions
of wisdom,
untold stories and
adventurous desires.

Show me the ocean
you contain inside you.
I know how to swim.

- *oceans* -

I want to be the hope
that illuminates your darkness.
I want my faith to radiate
from every pore of my being.
I want my love to shine so bright
that even the sun squints.

- squinting -

When she talks
about her passions,
her eyes light up
but also wander
into the distance like
she's walking into a daydream.
And if you're lucky,
she'll take you with her.

- lucky -

Rarely am I at a loss for words,
but every moment with him
leaves me speechless.

- speechless -

A sudden blizzard
I never expected.
You walked away;
I stood alone, rejected.

The coldness in your words
started to bite;
an avalanche of pain
left me paralyzed.

The chilling darkness of
depression took hold of me.
It left my heart frozen;
I couldn't breathe.

A scarf, coat, or gloves -
I had none.
And infinite clouds blocked
warmth from the sun.

It was in this moment
that I came to realize
the deepest level of Hell
is covered in ice.

- ninth circle -

Memories of you and I
danced together in the dark
like shadows on the wall,
only to disappear without a trace
as the sun peaked through the shades.

- shadows -

Just let me feel this pain.
Let me embrace it so
it absorbs through my skin
and flows through my veins.
Let it burn in my heart
and set my soul on fire.
Let the spark of doubt
and desperation become
an inferno of strength and hope.

- inferno -

Our love is changing
with the seasons.
Once hot with passion
like the summer sun,
now dead and dry
like the fallen leaves
of autumn.

- seasonal love -

I hope I'm the kind
of memory that makes you smile.

- good memories -

I learned to
smile again.

I learned to
laugh again.

I learned to
love again.

(I learned how to
live without you).

- lessons learned -

Love is never overrated —

love for God
love for self
love for others

None of it is overrated.

- *underrated* -

It's a little selfish how
you keep your walls up.
You have to let the world
discover how incredible you are.

It's not fair to keep that to yourself.

- selfish -

Captivating…
the way kindness
beams through his eyes
like sunlight splitting
through clouds in the sky.

- captivating -

The only hearts
meant to be played
are those in a deck of cards.

- queen of hearts -

There were times
I said, "I love you,"
too soon,
at the worst moment,
and without knowing
much about the person.

Still,
I have never
and will never
regret telling someone
I love them.

- no regrets -

I wish on stars and
get lost in dreams.
I believe in God,
true love,
and miracles,
and that is me.

- me -

You've always admired
my ability to fly,
but the truth is,
I've never had
a safe place to land.

- flying -

You've caged your heart
for far too long,
treating it like a prisoner
who committed no crime,
just in the wrong place
at the wrong time.

- prisoners -

When
Animosity
Rages
Relentlessy
I
Only
Rise

- *W.A.R.R.I.O.R* -

They say time
heals all wounds,
but what happens when
a wound freezes time?

- *wounded* -

Grabbing the knife from your hand,
the one you so desperately wanted to use,
I had to be the strong one
and do what you couldn't do.

Severing the bond
that tied our souls,
emptying myself of us,
love bleeding out on the floor.

Now you can tell everyone
how I butchered your heart
as you walk away…
…completely unscathed.

- severing souls -

And tonight,
the fireworks mock my pain.
Every BOOM echoes the shots
you aimed at my chest,
bursting my heart into
irreparable shards,
and burning out the
fiery sparks of love.

No vivid colors.

No brilliant lights.

Just,
smoke residue
and darkness
left behind.

- the fourth -

You were a master manipulator,
an expert at sleight of hand.
Love was your act and I was easily fooled
by your illusions of romance.

But your promises of forever
were simply a misdirection,
because "Abracadabra!"
just like that, you disappeared.

- houdini -

You are no longer
the love song
stuck in my head.

The melody has faded
from my lips
and my heart
has forgotten the lyrics.

- favorite song -

Every word I write
eliminates a piece of you
from my heart,
leaving you permanently
stranded on a page.
A page easily crumbled
and thrown in the trash.

- rough draft -

When so many men
end up disappointing you,
after a while, you don't
want to have feelings anymore.

And when your heart
gets broken enough times,
somewhere along the line,
you give up on the idea
that you deserve to fall in love.

- disappointment -

I was everything
he ever wanted…

… until he got to know me.

- *everything* -

I broke all my rules for you.
You were my exception,
and I was your fool.

- rules -

Her silhouette illuminated
by a glow through the pane,
while fingers trace odysseys
of tiny drops of rain.

Drowning in a sweater,
lost in a labyrinth of dreams,
or, maybe they're nightmares.
Nothing is ever what it seems.

Time stands still,
yet days fly by.
She now sees clearly
thanks to many tears cried.

She will not be defeated.
She will never give up.
No amount of heartbreak
will eliminate her belief in love.

- *silhouette* -

It's okay to cry and
let the hurt soak in,
but darling, remember
God never leaves you broken.

A new day is coming,
the sun will rise,
and eventually those tears
will dry from your eyes.

- rise -

I felt this darkness before.
I battled this darkness before.
I defeated this darkness before.

… and I will again.

- darkness defeated -

Hang
On and
Pray
Earnestly

- H.O.P.E -

After the world
broke me to pieces,
God brought me peace.

- peace -

God is the thread
that stitched my heart
back together.

- stitches -

I've sat in the ruins
of what was once called my life,
isolated and unsure where to begin again.
As a tear streamed down my cheek,
I bowed my head and prayed, "Please, help me."
and in that moment of complete destruction,
for the first time in a long time, I felt whole.

- whole -

Instead of dwelling
on your mistakes
and living with regret,
take that pain and use it.
Learn from it.
Transform into someone better.
Say, "I'm sorry," then prove it
by living your life in such a way,
you inspire others to become
the best versions of themselves.

- transformation -

You're allowed more
than one comeback
in a lifetime.

- *comeback* -

It's a little ridiculous
how we believe our mistakes
are powerful enough to ruin
God's plan for our lives.

- ridiculous -

People say
fairytales aren't real,
and as we grow up,
we start to believe that lie.

The truth is,
you can have
that kind of love,
we just give up on it.

- ever-after -

Why are you so eager
to give your love away?
Don't you see,
you need to save
some for yourself?

- keepsake -

Despite the chaos that defined her life
the countless broken hearts
and endless tears cried,
she always had a way of finding hope,
and that is how I knew a happy ending
would one day find her.

- happy ending -

I am an optimist
because I have traveled to
the darkest corners of my soul,
overstayed my welcome,
but still, somehow,
made it out alive.

- traveler -

I am nothing short
of a sequence of extremes
blended with idealistic expectations.

- *sequence* -

When you are near,
I feel calm.
I feel warmth.
My soul is lighter
and I am home.

- love -

You say I'm blind
since I am unable to see
your imperfections.
But if you could see
how bright you shine,
you'd be blinded too.

- blind -

My heart sees only you,
and my soul smiles at
the sound of your name.

- josh -

God designed your heart
so my soul would have
a place to call home.

- home -

I will give you all the words
and meaning you long for.
All I ask is for your touch
in its most innocent form.
For even your slightest graze
delights my soul and reignites
a fire inside I thought had died
long ago.

- delighted -

I could get used to you,
but never enough of you.

- in awe -

Stars burn with jealousy
in the night sky,
for the moon never
radiated love upon them
as bright as your love
shines for me.

- jealousy -

I'm not sure I can explain
exactly why I love you.
All I know is, my heart
has a hard time beating
when you're gone.

- explanation -

It's enchanting
the way your soul
intertwined with mine.

- enchanting -

You are not
of this world,
but many worlds —
a product of
magical encounters,
purest desires, and
the wildest daydreams.

- magical -

And with that kiss,
he brought the light
back to my eyes, and
a beat back to my heart.

- *kisses* -

And you, well,
you're special
for you

look like
taste like
smell like
feel like
sound like

all things love.

- all things love -

It was when I
looked into your eyes,
I had proof heaven existed.

- heaven -

I always thought true love
gave you amnesia to make you
forget past hurts, but I was wrong.
True love doesn't make you forget.

It makes you:
talk about it
overcome it,
heal it.

then looks at the scars
and says, "How beautiful!"

- amnesia -

I want to study your story
in its entirety, not just read it idly.
I want to bend corners,
highlight important parts,
and take notes in the margins.

Don't just show me
your favorite parts.
Show me everything,
and maybe I can help you
write the next chapter.

- a novel idea -

It's comforting,
knowing God is on my side,
even when I'm not.

- comforting -

She's been lied to, but
still knows how to trust.
She's been hurt, but
still knows how to love.
She's forgiving, but
knows how to move on.
Her ability to remain vulnerable
in spite of all the pain
is her greatest strength.

- vulnerable -

Even with your faults
you are still worth loving.

- worth it -

Sweet girl,
you lack nothing,
for God lives
in your heartbeat
and flows through
your veins.

- His image -

Watch out for Dimmers –
people who hold you back,
refuse to step up, and
prevent you from shining bright.
Let them go.

You are so much more
than a faint glow.
You were meant to
illuminate the world.

- dimmers -

It seems like my role
has come to an end.
I was meant to be a seasonal,
not a lifetime, friend.

I hope you know
how much you mean to me
and that I thoroughly enjoyed
being a part of your story.

- seasonal friends -

You're the one who
struck a match and
played with fire.

Don't blame me for your burns.

- burned -

And you hate me because
I choose to step into my light
and bloom without you.
It's not my fault
you refuse to grow.

- grow -

Even though it'd be easy
to label you the villain,

I'll choose to remember
the good parts of you.

- villain -

Bang! Bang! Bang!
You used your words
as a weapon.

Bang! Bang! Bang!
A rapid-fire of insults
designed to deteriorate
my self-worth.

Bang! Bang! Bang!
And when you emptied
your clip of all its rounds,
I walked away unscathed.

The bullets meant to destroy me
turned out to be just blanks.

- bullet proof -

Your soul
was as cold
as ice, and I
was without
a coat.

- brr -

She said, "I'm sorry," then
pulled her hand from his grasp
and walked away, but don't mistaken
her words as an apology for leaving.
It was her way of saying, "I pity you."
For how sad is it to not be able to
recognize love, even when you
hold it in your hands?

- apologies -

We wanted all the same things,
except I wanted them with you,
and you wanted them with her.

- intentions -

Sometimes,
letting go
is the best way
to show someone
you love them.

- sometimes -

I close my eyes,
hoping to escape sadness
for a little while, but
in my dreams you're
holding me again
kissing me again
in love with me again.

… and I wake up missing you more.

- imagination -

And as I lose sleep over him,
he sleeps while losing me.

- sleeping beauty -

I loved you with
a burning passion,
so, I guess I'm
the one to blame
for the inferno that
reduced my heart
to ashes.

- *ashes* -

It wasn't until we shared
all our secrets,
all our insecurities
all our dreams
that we became total strangers

- strangers -

For me,
it will always
be you,
even if for you
it won't always
be me.

- you -

I am done trying to compose
my own ever after.
I botched the storyline and
have scribbled out mistakes
too many times.

I relinquish my pen and
a mess of a draft to
the One who *is* love,
for He always creates
the perfect masterpiece.

- best-seller -

Your brokenness…
it is not permanent
it is not ugly
it is not shameful.

It is human
it is transitory.

You will heal, and
you will learn to
love yourself again.

- butterfly -

Sometimes it startles me,
sadness from my heart
leaking onto paper.
I thought I defeated the darkness,
but it's always lingering,
patiently waiting for my flame
of happiness to burn out.

And when it does,
I just have to remind myself
to strike another match.

… it's as easy and difficult as that.

- matches -

I refuse to become jaded.
I will not let the coldness
of others harden my heart.
I reject negativity and cynicism.
I will hold on to my hope and my faith.
I will respond to hate with love, always love.
And no matter how harsh life gets,
I will remain gentle, graceful, and a woman of God.

- repeat -

Life has a funny way
of helping us find people
we never knew we needed.

- friends -

You should be so energetic about life
that people are electrocuted by
your presence.

- electricity -

I will expire before
my optimism ever does.

    - optimist -

I am
beautiful,
strong,
sensitive,
unstoppable,
sometimes pitiful,
sometimes doubtful,
hopelessly romantic,
but mostly I am
pretty damn wonderful.

- wonderful -

Isn't it a wonderful thought,
that our paths could cross again in the future
and timing would be on our side?

- *timing* -

People change if you let them,
but if you keep reminding them
of who they used to be,
how do you expect them to
become who they are meant to be?

- *change* -

Though your heart was
beautifully designed,
it was not fashioned in a way
to love me the way I needed.

- polite rejection -

It's not that you weren't enough,
but maybe too much for him to handle.
Fear not, you will find a guy who
adores your too-muchness, and he
will be man enough to love you
the way you deserve.

- too much -

Is it really such
a crazy thought,
believing you deserve
to be loved in a way
that doesn't keep
you guessing?

- crazy thoughts -

In your old t-shirt
I've been sleeping,
and in my dreams
your memory
I'm keeping.

- t-shirt -

If words left
visible scars
do you think
we would choose
them more wisely?

- *wise words* -

And yes, the sun
still shines even when
you aren't here,
but my world is
a whole lot brighter
when you are near.

- proximity -

It took all the strength I possessed
to hold back that first tear, for I knew
it would lead to an unstoppable flood.

But my efforts were in vain.
That tear fell anyway.

Now I'm drowning –
I can't catch my breath and
I've forgotten how to swim.

- drowning -

I cried
over my unrealized expectations
over the lost illusion of potential
over who I thought you could be.

But don't be foolish,
not a single tear fell
for your true character.

- not one -

You used to wander
into my daydreams,
always as a pleasant
surprise.

But now, you haunt
my sleep, only meeting me
in my worst nightmares.

- *sleepless* -

Spare me from your
half-hearted promises and
false expectations of a future.

I am worth more.
I deserve more.

And this time,
I get to say,
what you have to offer
is not enough.

- not enough -

First, I wished for
you to notice me.
(And you did)

Next, I wished
you would love me.
(But you couldn't)

Then, I wished
to get over you.
(I did.)

And finally, my wishes
no longer have anything
to do with you.

- wishes -

I used to think of you
as my anchor,
but now I see
you've done nothing
but weigh me down.

- anchors away -

I thought losing you
would destroy the
exquisite portrait of us
painted by my mind's naivete.

Turns out, my perspective
was simply askew and
me without you is quite
the masterpiece.

- masterpiece -

Everyone seems to be
starving for love,
yet, here I am
offering my heart
and it's not enough to
satisfy anyone's appetite.

- starving -

Maybe someday
Happiness and I will be
close friends instead of
casual acquaintances.

- *acquaintances* -

Hope, answer me this:
Are you my sustaining breath,
or the reason for my
slow, agonizing death?

- breath -

I've had my fair share of storms
with raging winds that shook
the foundation I stood on,
and heavy downpours
that almost drowned me.

But I made it
out alive, and stronger.
And if the only purpose
of it all was to show you
the storms could be survived,
it was all worth it.

- storms -

It's okay if you hit rock bottom
and get stuck in a pit of despair.
Just don't stay stuck.
Don't sit there passively.
Don't accept defeat.

Find a way, *any* way, to get out.
Claw your way out,
kick, scream, cause a scene.

Better yet, call out for God.
He'll throw you a rope.

- *climbing* -

Closure —

the moment
after heartbreak
when you can
think of yourself,
and smile.

- closure -

Don't pity my broken heart,
for it always find a way to heal itself.

Instead, REJOICE!
For I got to experience
love once more.

- rejoice -

My world remained intact.
My optimism, preserved
and my romantic notions, protected.

My heart may have
a new scar or two,
but it still beats.
And life? It goes on.

- survivor -

For years, I have been
waiting on Superman
to come and save me.

But in the wait,
I discovered in me,
a Wonder Woman, and
I learned how to save myself.

- rescued -

When I prayed for love,
I trusted God would lead me there.

It was a pleasant surprise when
He led me to my own heart.

- answered prayers -

You deserve
to feel loved.
By others? Yes,
but most importantly,
yourself.

- self-love -

I will always lead you back to yourself
when life tricks you into believing
you are less than something special.

- *tricks* -

You are my friend.
Your battles are my battles.
And when life tries to attack,
I won't be fighting by your side.
I'll be leading the charge.

- battles -

Everyone has storms
they must weather in life,
but storms don't last forever.
Eventually, the rainbow
shines through and you find
you've bloomed.

- *bloom* -

There are no monsters
under the bed.
They found it better
to live in my head.

- monsters -

Tell me,
how can I
convince you
that you, exactly
as you are, are
more than enough?

- tell me -

The demons in my mind like
to battle the angels in my soul.
And though the demons
put up one hell of a fight,
I think it's important you know
the angels win every time.

- angels -

I hope my words
etch into your heart,
so even when you're alone,
you never forget you are loved.

- engraving -

Let me help
stitch your wounds
for I know how painful
it is to bleed.

- seamstress -

Isn't it exhausting,
being the only one
who can't see your shine?

- *exhausted* -

Don't let anyone
make you believe
you don't deserve
God's awesome plan
for your life.

- *destiny* -

You are beautiful.
You are worthy.
And darling, you are
far more than enough

- you are -

~~And maybe someday,~~
I'll learn to love my whole self,
even the parts that are broken.

- today -

They say my hope in love
will be my downfall,
but I'm not sure how
believing in love after
so much heartbreak
is anything short of a victory.

- *victory* -

You will find that
once-in-a-lifetime love
you long for, and it will be
greater than anything
you've ever imagined.

- once-in-a-lifetime -

And one of the
most beautiful things
in the world, I think,
is when broken hearts
learn to love once more.

- *once more* -

If you must give me a title
then call me "romantic,"
but please, never say
I'm "hopeless".

- hopeful -

People tell me I'm
obsessed with love,
as if it's a bad thing.
Of all the things
to be addicted to,
love is the best.

- addicted -

I live in a daydream —
a forever romantic in a
perpetual state of hope.

- forever romantic -

I still believe in chivalry
dresses that twirl
and that love is the
greatest thing in the world

- twirling dresses -

My prince is the
Prince of Peace.
The dragon he slays
is that of sin and death.
And happily-ever-after
is the day I join Him in paradise.

Don't tell me fairytales don't exist,
because I'm living one.

- fairytales -

Don't ever let
the jaded parts of you
speak louder than
the loving parts of you.

- loving parts -

I have several superpowers,
but optimism is, by far,
my most favorite.

- superpower -

Never stop seeing
the beauty in optimism.

Never stop hoping for
happily-ever-after.

Never stop believing
in the magic of love.

- *perseverance* -

Be soft, there is
beauty in that.

Be forgiving, there is
strength in that.

Be loving, for only
good will come of that.

Don't let the world
strip you of all the
wonderful things
that make you, you.

- pastel -

ACKNOWLEDGMENTS

I have to start by thanking my parents, Tom and Jan. You remind me how much I am loved when I feel weak and broken, and you constantly show me grace and forgiveness when I know I don't always deserve it. Thank you for showing me what it means to love unconditionally. Thank you for all your sacrifices so I could pursue various dreams throughout my life. Thank you for your steadfast belief in me. You are my strongest support system and my greatest blessing. I love you.

To my sisters, Jill and Kelly: I am so blessed to have sisters that support me so fiercely, not just with this book, but in life. Your loyalty and selflessness are inspiring. Thank you for always having my back, keeping me grounded, and my head above the water. You are my best friends; I love you.

To Micaela, my adorable 3-year-old niece and goddaughter: I hope you always believe in fairytales and happy endings. And please, never stop giving me running hugs, big kisses, and huge laughs.

To Connor, my equally adorable, 8-month-old nephew: You are so young and I am still getting to know you, but that smile of yours melts my heart and I absolutely love you.

To Baby-Girl Knebel, my unborn niece: I haven't met you yet, but I already know I'm incredibly in love with you. I hope to be a good example of God's love in your life.

To Grandma Gruber: Thank you for showing me how to overcome obstacles with poise and grace, and teaching me to always approach others with patience and love.

To Grandpa Gruber: Thank you for taking me fishing and making everyone wait to leave until I caught a fish. That long day taught me a valuable lesson in perseverance and optimism.

To Grandma Lange: Thank you for showing me how there is strength in being soft and humble.

To my friends Maddy, Sasha, Chris, and Adam: Thank you for always being there and showing up. Our late-night talks about relationships, our goals, and faith in God help re-center my heart on what matters most.

To Josh: You always believed in my dream of publishing this book, sometimes more than me, and you gave me the push I needed to finally see it to fruition. Thank you.

To Rosannae "Billy": Thank you for your designs and illustrations for this book. I would not have been able to publish as soon as I did without your talent and speedy delivery. You helped my dream come true.

To Morgan: Thank you for providing your photography services to help me create my marketing. Your advice and skill made it better than I imagined. (Instagram: @morganbethelphoto)

To lost loves and friendships: Thank you for letting me be a part of your life, if even for only a short while. You were valuable lessons learned.

Made in the USA
Monee, IL
05 December 2022

19793780R00085